D1592814

Also by Nicholas A. Virgilio

Selected Haiku, Burnt Lake Press and Black Moss Press, Canada, Second Edition, 1988

Selected Haiku, Burnt Lake Press, Quebec, Canada, 1985

About Nicholas A. Virgilio

Nick of Time . . . Nick of Time, a play by Joe Paprzycki

remembering Nick Virgilio, a film by Sean Dougherty

Other Turtle Light Press Haiku Titles

BIENNIAL HAIKU CHAPBOOK CONTEST PRIZEWINNERS

The Window That Closes, Graham High, 2013 *(forthcoming)*

All That Remains, Catherine J.S. Lee, 2011

Sketches from the San Joaquin, Michael McClintock, 2009

Haiku Abroad Collections

Peace and War: Collected Haiku from Israel, Rick Black, 2007

✻

Nick Virgilio: A Life in Haiku

Nicholas A. Virgilio

Nick Virgilio: A Life in Haiku

Edited and Introduced by Raffael de Gruttola

Afterword by Kathleen O'Toole

Turtle Light Press • Arlington, Va. • 2012

For Tony Virgilio and the Nick Virgilio Haiku Association members,
all of whom have helped keep Nick's poetry alive

Table of Contents

Preface

It was at the Haiku North America conference in 2009 that I first learned of a large archive of unpublished haiku left behind by Nick Virgilio. I had admired Nick's work for years. Having been a reporter for *The New York Times* in the Middle East, I found that his poems resonated deeply and helped me deal with all of the violence that I had encountered. I found particularly meaningful his haiku about the death of his youngest brother Larry in Vietnam.

Soon after the conference, I contacted Tony Virgilio, Nick's middle brother, in order to introduce myself and talk to him about publishing a new collection of Nick's poems. He liked the idea and, a few months later, I took a first look at Nick's papers, which were being kept in the English department of Rutgers University in Camden, N.J.

In a black metal filing cabinet, I discovered reams of legal-size papers, all covered with drafts of poems in various forms: haiku, sonnets, and some longer verse. Notes were scribbled in margins. Randomly, I took out a handful of papers and started reading the poems:

New Year's morning . . .
among many in the drawer,
a few bright pennies

And a Vietnam haiku that I had never seen:

summer nightfall:
dazed, all I heard from the Major
". . . killed in Vietnam . . ."

And various versions of this poem:

over the city,
the shadow of the falcon
follows the pigeon

It would be a huge job to pick out the best ones, but Raffael de Gruttola — a haiku poet, former president of the Haiku Society of America and longtime admirer of Nick's poetry — graciously offered to take on the task. Additionally included in this volume are excerpts of a radio interview with Nick on WHYY, two articles by Nick on writing haiku, several essays, photos and more.

For those who are not yet acquainted with the images and emotions expressed so poignantly and powerfully in Nick's poems, I hope this collection will serve as a fitting introduction to one of this country's leading haiku poets. And for those readers who are already familiar with his work, I hope this volume will reawaken and deepen their love of his haiku.

Rick Black, Publisher
Arlington, Virginia

Introduction

Nick Virgilio was a genuine pioneer of American haiku poetry. Born and bred in Camden, New Jersey, where his idol, Walt Whitman, retired and is buried, Nick decided in high school that he wanted to write poetry, and after serving in the Navy and working as a radio announcer, he pursued his dream. It wasn't until the early 1960s, however, that he became a full-time haiku poet.

He was first introduced to this Japanese genre after reading Kenneth Yasuda's book, *a pepper pod*, and spent countless hours alone in his cellar before his Remington typewriter producing hundreds of haiku from his daily walks throughout Camden and south Philadelphia. As we read his haiku today in this first American edition of his work, we find an almost monk-like approach in pursuit of the deepest moments of his life. His unique haiku written in 1963:

lily:
out of the water . . .
out of itself

captured a subtle awareness that the great Japanese haiku poets, from Basho to Santoka, knew all along. It was possible to say more with less. He wrote about nature and his family as well as about the lives of the people of Camden, N.J., a small city across the river from Philadelphia that was doing well in his youth but slowly went downhill in ensuing years as factories closed, drugs proliferated and crime became rampant.

During this deterioration of Camden, the Virgilio family suddenly felt the shock of reality when their youngest son, Lawrence, who joined the Marines to serve his country, was killed in Vietnam. The family, which went from hope to despair in confronting Larry's loss, had to deal with the ultimate sacrifice; it was devastating to them. It was about this time that Nick's haiku became solemn and elegiac. He attempted to deal with this tragedy by writing haiku as a healing process:

deep in rank grass,
through a bullet-riddled helmet:
an unknown flower

Here, the analogy with Whitman becomes important, for Nick saw in his haiku the circumstances that Whitman felt after the devastation of the Civil War. This pathos, if you will, becomes a constant reminder for Nick that one's life can be transformed if there is the will to believe in yourself and in your art. It's through this search and belief that Nick became the great haiku poet that we know today.

Rod Willmot, the Canadian editor of the first two collections of Nick's haiku, mentions that "the best haiku technique is usually invisible, and what looks easy as pie has been cooked with consummate skill." I have just completed reviewing more than 3,000 haiku written by Nick. His dedication to perfecting this short poem was constant. At times, he would revise and rewrite his first impressions in numerous ways to find just the right nuance. Often I read these mostly unknown haiku and then found on another page two or three slight changes, all of which were insightful new perceptions of nature.

Another issue was how often Nick crafted haiku that adhered to a 5-7-5 syllable count, which was popular at first among haiku poets writing in English. The more I reviewed and questioned this approach, the more I saw that Nick had an uncanny take on the sounds of syllables and could find new meanings in unique uses of simple words and phrases. In later years, Nick wasn't so intent on counting syllables. Rather, he was more interested in the essential meaning and resulting emotion that each line of the haiku exhibited:

the long winding road:
a run-over rattlesnake
writhing in the sun

Here, the first line reflects the image of a snake, immediately juxtaposed by its uncoiling in death. Other thoughts emerge even from the first line that speaks, if you will, of the journey that one takes through life. Haiku poets often retain the sound or meaning of a perceived moment for a long time until they have captured the exact picture that they want to use to recreate a particular feeling.

Nick often paraphrased Professor Harold Henderson's classic book, *Haiku in English*, about what a haiku is: "If the reader doesn't see the picture, that is, the proper picture-composition before feeling the emotion, then much of the effect is lost. Haiku are not puzzles, but picture-poems." Nick's haiku, at times, also use internal rhyme or sounds that play off one another in original, meaningful ways.

Many of his haiku reflect his daily routine. He usually rose early and had breakfast at the Elgin Diner, then went for lengthy walks along various paths and trails, sometimes late into the night to record those moments in time that he wrote about in his haiku. He often stopped at the Sacred Heart Church and asked the pastor, Father Michael Doyle, or other unsuspecting souls for their opinions of his haiku. In selecting the haiku to include in this new edition, I have tried to chronicle Nick's life in his daily routines.

In ordering the poems, I have also used a technique that early Japanese poets would use when they met collaboratively to compose renku, a linked form of poetry that pre-dates the development of the haiku. Basically, one haiku can reverberate with or against another. For example, the following two haiku:

hospital quiet
I enter alone at twilight:
the scent of lilacs

now the swing is still:
a suspended tire
centers the autumn moon

The relationship of the first haiku to the second may not seem obvious at a glance, but after a few seconds it's evident that the situation presented in the juxtaposition can be immediate, if one realizes that the autumn moon in the Japanese haiku tradition is a "season" word for the moments before passing from one world to the next.

While Nick died in 1989, his poetry is still cherished and read around the world. These poems are as alive and vibrant today as when he first penned them — and, incredibly, just as relevant. This collection of new, mostly unpublished haiku — with a number of classics from the two earlier collections — is an attempt to make known today to both old fans and newcomers alike the breadth and power of his poetry.

I hope this new edition of Nick Virgilio's haiku will firmly establish his legacy as one of America's premier haiku poets and help readers understand the power of the haiku as a poetic form and why it has become popular not only in the United States but throughout the world.

Raffael de Gruttola
Natick, Massachusetts

Haiku

my brother and I
in the old cemetery
reading epitaphs

in the empty church
at nightfall, a lone firefly
deepens the silence

autumn twilight . . .
corn stalks creaking in the wind,
the taste of cider

hot summer field:
a killdeer's cry
awakens the child

evening sun
on the back of the bullfrog:
dragonfly

the gliding eagle
adds another shape of shadow
to the mountain

signing myself out
of the Coronary Ward:
the sun on the lawn

ever present
in the cicada's cry:
hot summer

on the other end
of the kite —
a pigtailed girl

diploma in hand
sure she thinks the world
owes her a living

fog curls
through the field:
a snake in the morning grass

the incoming tide:
a tiny crab emerges
from a deep footprint

sticky heat . . .
tiny caterpillar wriggling
on a thread of air!

Memorial Day:
staring at the grassy plot
set aside for me

telegram in hand,
the shadow of the marine
darkens our screen door

autumn twilight:
the wreath on the door
lifts in the wind

between the tear drops
on the letter —
spring rain

deep in rank grass,
through a bullet-riddled helmet:
an unknown flower

in memory of Lawrence J. Virgilio

a skylark's song
and a billowing cloud
fills my emptiness

autumn nightfall,
recalling the Holocaust:
numbers on his arm

during the sermon
slipping out of a dark cloud:
the Passover moon

the morning mist:
dew hangs
from the spider's web

in the old pond
beside the monk's reflection
the autumn moon

in the empty church
a quiet child watching
flickering candles

the shaft of light:
a red-winged blackbird
perched on a pampas plume

among the rows and rows
of white crosses
patches of young grass

an old scarecrow —
for a moment
forgetting my loneliness

beneath pear blossoms
a swarm of red ants cover
the baby robin

by a dump
composing poems:
fireflies

my father and I
quarreling face to face
exchange breath

a dancing kite . . .
an audience of birds
clamoring for spring

the young leaves blown
this way, that way
spring moon

cherry blossoms . . .
lying on the sidewalk,
spattered by rain drops

against the seawall,
sweeping the Normandy beach:
chill fall winds

spring wind:
the child in uniform
returns my salute

behind
fighting fishmongers —
the flaring volcano!

reading at the tomb
mingling with the scent of lilac
the *Song of Myself*

lily:
out of the water . . .
out of itself

after the bell,
within the silence:
within myself

the autumn moon
awakens the baby
on the orphanage steps

a Wall Street winter:
the skyscraper's windows
corner the morning sun

sitting on a jetty . . .
watching a seagull
float on a thermal

my father and I
with no footprints to follow
step into deep snow

Easter alone
leaving her aged mother
in the nursing home

approaching the pond . . .
concentric ripples center
the mouth of the carp

the aging diva
    playing *Madame Butterfly*
        stares at the empty seats

at the White House steps,
begging for recognition:
Vietnam vets

taking my picture
with the cardboard president:
this Election Day

the sack of kittens
sinking in the icy creek
increases the cold

tenement roof:
tilted TV antenna
touches the moon

Vietnam monument
mirroring cherry blossoms
and gold star mothers

my palsied mother,
pressing my forehead on hers
this Ash Wednesday

sixteenth autumn since:
barely visible grease marks
where he parked his car

the long winding road:
a run-over rattlesnake
writhing in the sun

after the spring storm . . .
the farm girl washes her hair
in the rain barrel

pigeons in the park
gather at the empty bench:
the funeral bell

down the ghetto street
glittering with broken glass . . .
a barefoot child

touching her son's face
with her hands in the moonlight:
the blind woman smiles

the old cracked bell
rings with black children's laughter . . .
this Independence Day

bitter cold wind
carving a frozen snowdrift —
the crescent moon

silent World Series:
deaf mutes arguing over
the play at the plate

on the empty beach
beyond space shuttle fragments:
the cross in the sand

outside the meeting
of the Bible Society —
the slave auction

at the mine entrance,
on time cards beneath the clock:
the names of the dead

a bittern booms —
the harsh cry of a marsh hawk,
the crescent moon

Easter morning:
finishing up Communion wine
in the sacristy

filling the silence
on the long distance telephone:
the things unsaid

the blind musician
extending an old tin cup
collects a snowflake

the far line of trees
  and the river bridge beyond
    connecting cities

shadowing hookers
after dark:
the cross in the park

sick room window:
cicadas in the sycamore
serenade the child

autumn afternoon
father turning cold and grey:
I arrive too late

in the dead tree,
shadowing the frozen snow:
cemetery crows

entering the grove
now sanctified by the grave:
the scent of incense

autumn nightfall:
my mourning mother hears
little brother call

flag-covered coffin:
the shadow of the bugler
slips into the grave

atop the town flagpole,
a gob of bubblegum
holds my dead brother's dime

my little brother
with a spider in his hand:
a gift for mother

morning sun
on the foggy moor:
becoming a child

always returning
to the flag-covered coffin:
dragonfly

my spring love affair:
the old upright Remington
wears a new ribbon

the recess bell rings —
the teacher's chalk wears down
to a period.

following the parade
for Gay Liberation:
tiger swallowtail

barefooted lovers . . .
pulling the boat ashore —
leaving the moon afloat

in the night woods . . .
a lone candle lights the face
of the frightened child

early autumn cool:
a falling leaf's shadow
on the pebbled path

rising and falling . . .
a blanket of blackbirds feeds
on the snowy slope

the feuding neighbors
leaves and litter fraternize
in the bitter wind

no autumn moon
to hang
a verse on

the organ grinder
takes the monkey off his back:
the heat

Thanksgiving alone:
ordering eggs and toast
in an undertone

on the bedroom floor,
tying the umbilical cord:
March snowstorm

        for my father

having come this far
alive at fifty-five:
the morning star

ringing the church bell
for the Farm Workers' Mass:
the rope burn

on the petition
condemning Agent Orange:
the names of the dead

New Year's Eve:
pay phone receiver
dangling

on the cardboard box
holding the frozen wino:
Fragile: Do Not Crush

for Father Michael Doyle

the old neighborhood
falling to the wrecking ball:
names in the sidewalk

not a breath of air
in the crowded cathedral:
the sermon on Hell

monastic silence
in and out of a sunbeam:
buzzing horsefly

from the willow
it fell into the empty grave:
cicada shell

bass
picking bugs
off the moon

this golden maple
lifts
a heavy heart

in the young grass
a fledgling jay and a worm
stare at each other

darkened pool room:
a lone, shaded lamp dangles
in the dust and smoke

on my father's wrist,
keeping time and eternity:
my dead brother's watch

spentagon
pentagony
repentagon

an empty dory
    heaving on the bay — the heat
        of drum fish beneath

twilight
    and spring rain . . .
        one in the other

the afterglow
   beyond the blooming mimosa—
     a flight of redwings

city skyline in haze:
   the stench of the river—
     August dog days

the lake . . .
   an oil-slick slips over the dam:
   the rainbow

autumn cumulus: I found myself!

from rose thorn
to rose thorn:
a hailstone

over spatterdocks,
turning at corners of air:
dragonfly

the flowering hedge:
a dead horsefly
on the window ledge

on the manuscript
the shadow of a butterfly
finishes the poem

above the cloud peak
below the summer moon —
a flight of snow geese

hospital quiet
I enter alone at twilight:
the scent of lilacs

for Richard Wilbur

now the swing is still:
a suspended tire
centers the autumn moon

an old cemetery . . .
cobwebbed hedge in the morning mist
a distant bell

alone in my room . . .
I look up from a death verse —
my looming shadow

in the wet
  mimosa tree
    bats hanging

the long road:
walking with myself —
the summer heat

Afterword: An Echo in Time

Twenty-three years after his death, Nick Virgilio's haiku still echo for me like a voice reverberating in a deepening canyon. What is it in Nick's haiku that makes them so memorable? I have long mulled over this question. As a friend of Nick's and a member of the board of the Nick Virgilio Haiku Association, I have often been asked to share my reflections on Nick's legacy. The poems in this collection — some familiar, but many new and surprising — gave me the chance to rediscover their power and, perhaps, a hint of his enduring legacy in American haiku.

I first met Nick Virgilio in Camden, New Jersey, in 1983. As a friend and aspiring poet back then, I delighted in the 6 a.m. phone calls as his first collection debuted and was reviewed on National Public Radio, rejoiced as his voice reached new audiences through NPR and the celebrated publication of his *Selected Haiku* in 1988, and grieved when he died in early 1989. I was honored to have been asked to help Nick's brother Tony sort through Nick's papers — boxes of correspondence, scraps of haiku-in-progress on the back of church song sheets and cash register receipts, and hundreds of legal-sized sheets of typed, mostly unpublished haiku. Leaving Nick's basement workspace, I always felt like I was exiting a chapel, so palpable the devotion of the poet to his art.

So, is it my first-hand knowledge of how he wrote and rewrote, wrestled with the words, sometimes for years, to capture the exact emotion of a moment in images that makes the poems in *Selected Haiku* still ring in my ears two decades later? Having heard him read on many occasions and having listened to recordings of his readings and radio interviews, could it be that his *actual voice* — its resonant baritone cadence — has imprinted *lily, bass* and *the blind musician* in my memory like few other haiku in the decades since?

Reading and rereading this new broad selection of Nick's haiku, I have settled on three qualities that make them memorable to me, and ensure, as Cor van den Heuvel asserted at the time of Virgilio's death, that Nick's haiku would ". . . endure the changes of taste and time . . .": (1) the quality of the moment of perception; (2) Nick's powerful sense of place; and (3) the music of his haiku.

First, the moment. When asked to define haiku, Nick almost always started with "a moment of emotion, keenly felt. . .," or "emotion expressed at the sensory level." His best haiku capture exactly that, a deeply felt *moment* of perception. The images, or juxtaposition of images — fresh, odd, often humorous, occasionally disturbing — nearly always "grab me," to paraphrase his question when testing out his own haiku on friends: *How does that grab ya'?*

sixteenth autumn since:
barely visible grease marks
where he parked his car

74

my father and I
quarreling face to face
exchange breath

The keen emotion of these moments and the way in
which small detail, perceived and then rendered in "word
paintings" — Nick always compared himself to Buson
rather than Basho in describing his craft — will ensure that
these poems endure.

Second, the sense of place. Nick is often recognized as an
urban poet, for it is in the neighborhoods of Camden that he
is most grounded, in its industrial past and its tragic decay
of recent decades. But his sense of place is just as acute
returning to his grandfather's farm of memory, or in the
larger landscapes of his imagination.

shadowing hookers
after dark:
the cross in the park

barefooted lovers . . .
pulling the boat ashore —
leaving the moon afloat

Finally, the music. Nick was a jazz aficionado, lover of
the popular American songbook, who penned lyrics him-
self. As Raffael de Gruttola has noted, Nick has a special
knack for capturing the rhythms of ordinary speech in a
memorable way, leading to what might be critiqued as

'excess' words or syllables through the lens of today's preference for the sparest haiku (the likes of his *lily* and *bass* gems included here). Having noticed for myself the "ear echoes" of my favorite Virgilio haiku, I would agree with those who have praised Nick's word play and metric impulse — the intuitive link between sound and image, as he molded the Japanese haiku into a twentieth century American art form. And knowing him, I would guess: he just couldn't resist!

But close your eyes and listen:

the feuding neighbors
leaves and litter fraternize
in the bitter wind

— without the edge of sound, the irony and humor of the poet's perception would be lost.

in the dead tree,
shadowing the frozen snow:
cemetery crows

atop the town flagpole,
a gob of bubble gum
holds my dead brother's dime

— long vowels, short plosive syllables, nailing the emotion of the moment.

And the rhyming, riffing joy of . . .

> having come this far
> alive at fifty-five:
> the morning star

The music is integral to the perception and interpretation of Nick's experience, every bit as essential, I believe, to his art as the elegiac beauty of his Vietnam-era poems. My hope is that this new collection and his unique voice will touch many who have not heard it, with its invocation to write haiku " *'cause you might have a great poem in ya'. You never know . . . .*"

Kathleen O'Toole
Takoma Park, Maryland

An Interview With Nick

The Quick In Us: An Interview with Nick Virgilio
Marty Moss-Coane, WHYY, Philadelphia

Marty: With me now is poet Nick Virgilio. He's called by many this country's foremost haiku poet. He lives across the river in Camden, a place he's lived his whole life. Nick Virgilio is a consultant at the Walt Whitman International Poetry Center, which he helped to found in 1974 . . . . [Nick,] why have you chosen that particular form of poetry for yourself, a haiku?

Nick: Well, I accidentally stumbled on the haiku in the Rutgers library in 1963. I was looking for some Chinese verse and ran across Kenneth Yasuda's *a pepper pod*. I liked the verse and I tried a few, and I sent 'em off to a magazine advertising in *The Saturday Review* and they took one poem [in *American Haiku*, Issue 1, 1963]. And the first poem, which is the mother of all the poems which I've written, is:

Spring wind frees
  the full moon tangled
    in leafless trees

And then I won first prize in the next issue with the "lily" poem that I wrote, and first prize in the next issue, and then I built an international reputation from there.

Marty: But there must be something about choosing so few words to express yourself that you find satisfying.

Nick: Well, you know, I'm not that well read, really. And I'm not really intellectual . . . I'm an artist. And I found the thing that's my thing, and I do it, that's all. And I'm kind of like on the fringe of fringe as far as the poetry community is concerned. I don't care. I think my stuff is good. And if I . . . sooner or later pass on I'll leave something behind. Maybe one or two or three poems might help . . . somebody along the way, ya know.

Marty: You know what I find interesting . . . you are a talkative person. In person, I mean, you have a lot to say, and yet you've chosen as a form of expression poetry that is very untalkative. . . .

Nick: Hmmm, it's a paradox, isn't it? But, in not using literary allusions and things like that you more or less have to give the reader the quintessential experience, and that's what I do . . . I try to do. It's like the Christ child, I like to liken it to, you know. We all have that essence. You have an essence in you — and we let that shine through us. This is the quick of us, and this is the best part of us, and that's what I try to bring forth in my work.

Marty: How do you begin to choose the words? I know it's

always hard to ask artists, writers, painters how they do what it is that they do. But do you start with, for instance, an image? Your poetry is very visual.

Nick: Yeah . . . sometimes I'm inspired by people. Like a friend of mine said, "I want you to write something about how these women put their lipsticks on in the jukebox mirror in a diner." So, that challenged me, and I wrote this poem the other day:

applying eyeliner
in the jukebox mirror
the midnight diner

See, that's right on. It hits a contemporary nerve. If you could write 50 like that, you're out of sight, ya know. But ah, so, it varies. Sometimes you'll write a poem, very rarely, right off the bat. Like I was walking near the Elgin Diner in Camden. I looked over and saw the Walt Whitman Bridge and I wrote this:

the far line of trees
   and the river bridge beyond
      connecting cities

That's a landscape poem, see. And that's the only time I ever wrote a poem just like that. Most of 'em is rewriting and rewriting. My brother's poem, his funeral, took 15 years. It happened in '67; I wrote this in '82:

flag-covered coffin:
the shadow of the bugler
slips into the grave

Marty: The poems about your brother are particularly
moving and very, very sad. And I would like to have you
read kind of a series of them because they go in sequence
and you really take us through his death and your mourning
of his death.

Nick: Might tear me up though, hang in there.

Marty: Okay.

Nick:

deep in rank grass,
through a bullet-riddled helmet:
an unknown flower

Now this was inspired by the siege of Khantien, Vietnam,
September, 1967. There was a cliché picture in *The Courier
Post* showing a bullet-shattered helmet with . . . like a thorny
weed sticking through it. And it was like on [St.] Augustine
grass. So what I did is I grabbed that immediately and put
it on rank grass and three months later I got the last line.
So the first two lines were:

deep in rank grass,
through a bullet-riddled helmet

Then I was near Robins' Bookstore where it used to be on 13th and, you know, where's it . . . Filbert. And I was talking to somebody and all of a sudden the last line came right through my mind and it completed the poem. It was published in *Leatherneck Magazine* [in 1968].

Marty: And what's the last line:

Nick: An unknown flower.

deep in rank grass,
through a bullet-riddled helmet:
an unknown flower

I didn't like the poem originally because I thought the word bullet-riddled was a cliché.

Marty: Yeah.

Nick: But I found out that when you take a cliché and it becomes part of living language it's no longer a cliché.

This one took 20 years:

telegram in hand,
    shadow of the marine
        darkens our screen door

The marine waited two hours in the car for my mother

85

and father to come home. I waited til they were all seated and then I went out to the porch and motioned for him to come over, and he came over, and I will never forget that shadow coming on the screen. He had the telegram.

Marty: You, you knew he was there. And you were waiting.

Nick: I got the news first . . . it's like getting hit with a baseball bat. [long pause]

the autumn wind
has torn the telegram and more
from mother's hand

'Course it happened in the summer time . . . this is taking liberty on the experience.

into the blinding sun . . .
    the funeral procession's
        glaring headlights

[This] was written in 1964 from an entirely different experience, but the editor deemed it, ah, you know, appropriate to put it in the series. One I just wrote a few years ago:

removing the shroud:
    mother and father alone
        step out of the crowd

You see the rhyme's inevitable. It doesn't attract attention away from the substance of the poem.

beneath the coffin
at the edge of the open grave:
the crushed young grass

That's written for the next-door neighbor's son who was killed in a train crash . . . crushed . . . he was in the cab, and the caboose and another train come up and crushed him. So I wrote that for him. But it fits in here, too.

Here's one that really grabs me. The sergeant who recruited my brother, Sergeant Sphinx, he unwrapped the coffin and put the rifle shells in the coffin . . . and he had so much anguish on his face, it was [as] if his own son died. He handed it to my mother and father . . . this flag.

my gold star mother
and father hold each other
and the folded flag

The next is one of the best poems in the book. If I could write 50 like this . . . outta sight. Believe me:

Thanksgiving dinner:
  placing the baby's high chair
    in the empty space

See how universal that is? Then, the next one . . . these are autobiographical but there's a combination of imagined reality with it too:

on the darkened wall
  of my dead brother's bedroom:
    the dates and how tall

I never did that, but . . . something that's apropos, and I wrote it . . . but it took many years. You know what the original was? Listen to the original . . . how bad:

on the darkened wall
  of my dead brother's bedroom:
    pencil marks how tall

Marty: Hmmm.

Nick: Doesn't work.

Marty: No.

Nick: When you say the dates and how tall . . . you see.

Marty: Well, you feel the time going by.

Nick: Yeah . . . you feel time and you also can think of a tombstone . . . with the dates.

Marty: Were these poems cathartic for you . . . I mean

was this a way for you to . . . to . . .

Nick: Well . . . to get in touch with . . . the real . . . Like I said, the war never ended in our house until my mother died. And we took care of my mother the last nine years . . . and we were grieving all the time . . . and I was always full of emotion. My mother had Parkinson's disease. Which was very bad, and she . . . my mother. My mother gave up when my brother died because she felt that he died for nothing and who could tell her different. See. And she gave up and she got Parkinson's and she finally died and now she's at peace.

[Long pause.]

My father died taking care of my mother . . . before his time. So I'm telling everybody . . . don't go to war . . . because a war'll never end. And we have it easy compared to the MIAs and the paraplegics. The war'll *never* end for them. Nothing to do with John Wayne. Has everything to do with reality and the horrors of war. I been trying to write a poem now for years. When my . . . my ma . . . the week before my brother died in Vietnam my mother was . . . was looking in the mirror and she was crying. I said, "Mother". . . I was perturbed . . . I said, "Mom, what's the matter?" She turned around and looked at me . . . that's all . . . just looked at me.

Marty: There were no words?

Nick: She knew where he was. She felt that. And I wrote this. I haven't been able to get the last line:

turning from the mirror
terror and tears in her eyes

. . . but I haven't gotten the last line yet . . . It's been over 21 years I've been working on that.

Marty: And a poem like that for you needs a last line?

Nick: Well, not for me, but for the reader it does. To make it objective and universal, you know I have to — I could say "the marine's mother." I couldn't say "my gold star mother." I've got to — I can't use any abstraction or summation in the last line. You see, the haiku is against any sort of a tag title or any kind of a title at all. You can't use the intellect on the surface of the poem. It's got to be poetry of the five senses that makes you feel first and think about it afterwards, you see. You can't tell the reader . . .

May I read this please, about the cats — I wrote this in '67:

the sack of kittens
  sinking in the icy creek
    increases the cold

Note how we get the real feeling of winter — not visual

and picturesque, but tactile cold and kinesthetic sinking. The chill is felt not in the intellect but in skin and bone. Emotion is expressed on the sensory level — this is the essence of haiku. Emotion expressed on the sensory level. Moreover, repeated reading of the poem and meditation on it, reveal many layers of meaning: one form of existence passes into another, warmth into cold, living into non-living, the organic returns to the inorganic. We, too, are involved in this eternal transition; we too are in the sack sinking in the icy creek. The doctrine of Mahayana Buddhism holds that life and the individual are merely temporary manifestations of being . . . .

It is this linking of human nature to all nature, this illumination of our being through a simple experience expressed in simple images that endow haiku poetry with unique depth and meaning. This is very important because of the ecological problems that we have. That we're not in touch with nature and it's high time we did.

Marty: And you feel that your poetry does that, or all poetry does?

Nick: Well, I wouldn't be presumptuous to say that my poetry does but I think that we should. We cannot be reactionary and go back pre-Industrial Revolution but we've got to get back to the earth somehow. We wear shoes, we got rugs under here — we never touch the earth.

My grandfather before he died picked up a clod of earth

and said, "You think you're better than this?" You see?
We're made of the earth. We should get back to the earth
— and that means that we can't, like I said, we can't be
reactionary. We haven't survived the Industrial Revolution.
You know. It's a cliché. It's the truth, though, we haven't.

Marty: You know, you talk about being in touch with the
earth, and it makes me think that you use a World War II
typewriter, and that the idea of touching a typewriter like
that is that you really have to work your hands.

I mean, do you feel, in a way, that the poems really
come through your fingers? The way, I suppose, that one
of these computers doesn't give you.

Nick: No, no, not really . . . I think it would be phony for
me to say that. I just write, you know. I write 'cause I have
to write. I was turned on by the "lily" poem. People said,
"Man, you're good, you've got talent," you know. And it
becomes like a disease after a while — you keep writing,
and you become good at it, so, here you are — you build
a better mousetrap, and people beat a path to your door,
you know, so . . . . So what's it all mean, really? What can
you be? A tight little package of humanity. You can explore
this provincial you and become the universal. And that's
all. And then if you become this tight little package of
humanity, you have something to offer. You really have
something to offer — yourself, and that's all you have to
offer anyway. I try to do that through my work.

Marty: What keeps you in Camden? And I guess people don't think of poets living in Camden [or even] know that Walt Whitman was there but . . . but certainly it's a city that has died. Perhaps it's coming back to life . . . but why are you still there?

Nick: I traveled all over the country and I wasn't creative. I've lived in New York and all. I was . . . I'm creative at that home at 1092 Niagara Road, and if I leave that home, I'm not creative any more. I got roots there. I'm kind of a Cancer, I'm a Cancer person. A home-body. And my brother, he wants to sell the house . . . after Mom died, because he's really in grief, too. I can understand it. I said, "This is not a house to me, this is my home."

Marty: And this a home you've grown up, your whole life?

Nick: Thirty-nine, since '39 I've been there. I lived in Camden, I lived in the slums when I was a kid, you know . . . common-law wives and bootleggers . . . and we had a nice home, and we didn't have that much, got a dime spendin' money a week, a dollar for Christmas, you know . . . ate pretty good, and my mother made her own clothes. My mother made dresses you could wear inside-out, and in clothes, she was very good, very good.

I want to read something I wrote for her. It's not a haiku, but I'd like to give her a tribute. When I was a kid, 1935, I was in second grade. The school teacher said,

"We're going to have a schoolyard play with a Dutch motif." And I said, "Who's going to be the master of ceremonies?" She thought that was so cute, and she said, "Well, you're going to be the master of ceremonies." So, I went home to my mother. She wasn't that educated. There was no TV, no magazines. I said, "Mom, I need a microphone." We used to listen to John Facenda on the radio in the early '30s. So this is what she did.

My ingenious mother alone
fashioned a homemade microphone
from two tops of soft boxes
two disks of wire screen
fitted with glue . . .

Marty: . . . You all right? [responding to Nick's choking up]

Nick:

to a broom handle
in the base of a basket
to stand in place,
fashioned a little MC.

The second-grader took his cue
and introduced the schoolyard play
of Holland in the month of May.

With boys and girls in Dutch costumes
and wooden shoes

94

tulips in bloom
everything came alive
in the spring of 1935.

[pauses, Virgilio's voice breaks...]

Marty: So your poems —

Nick: Maybe I shouldn't have read it . . .

Marty: So your poems really are your life, I mean, in a
way, it's your, it's your story, I guess it's the story of your
family —

Nick: Well, I had to write that verse. Wrote it in '74 or
'75, that's forty years afterwards. I believe what Words-
worth says about "emotion recollected in tranquility."
That's what that is. A high point in my life, one of the high-
est points. So I wrote that for her. It was published, and it
came out very naturally, you know. And that's what —
they have to come out like babies. We don't like artificial-
ity in our art, we don't want it. Like with what Keats said,
if it doesn't come out naturally, it better not come at all.

Marty: Do you find that in reading your poems that you
then re-live the emotion that goes into it? I mean, it seems
like you don't have a lot of defenses against your feelings.

Nick: You've got to be a kind of masochist, I think, to be a poet, in a way.

Marty: Do you feel that?

Nick: Well, no, not really. I don't know. There are no absolutes in a relative world, so there must be a bit of masochism in me. And I hope that I got more than sadism, or whatever's the opposite, you know. Yeah, well, the thing is, I try to make my life count for something. We all have these tragic experiences, and life basically is tragic, nobody lives happily ever after. So what I hope to do is to uplift it and bring it into the realm of beauty, and I agree with that, because a lot of my great poems, I say that "great" — great to me, quote, are about death, you see. And Whitman wrote about death — there's a great beauty in death; there's a great resolution; there's a great peace in it.

Marty: Is Whitman an inspiration for you? I mean, he's a fellow Camden —

Nick: Well, I love Whitman's poetry, but I can't say I write anything like him. Whitman packs words in, and I take 'em away, simplistically speaking. And he's a great poet, he's a visionary — I'm not a great poet, I'm a good poet, but I'm not a great poet, you know, and Whitman, you know, he's a visionary, he's — well, like with Whitman, he's — I mean, if you want to study nineteenth century America, you've got to read Walt Whitman's *Leaves of Grass*. He's not only a poet, he's a historian, too . . . .

Marty: You know, it's so interesting to me, and so wonderful, in a way, that poetry so delicate as yours can survive in a town like Camden.

Nick: Well, look, to survive, man, is a miracle anyway for any one of us. There's always something trying to put you in the coffin. Thursday — let me tell you what happened Thanksgiving, three days before my mother died. I ended up in a hospital. I ate too much, and I thought I was going to die . . . and if it wasn't for George [Vallianos, proprietor of the Elgin Diner] and some of my friends, I might've died, right out there on the street. I got in there, and then I wrote this poem:

ending Thanksgiving
in the emergency ward
among the living

That's my poem of gratitude for surviving that. I've had a lot of trouble this last year with congestive heart failure. I had two heart attacks in the last eight years. It's a wonder that I'm alive, really. And, plus anxiety, you know, there's such, there's so much that goes with it. Go ahead.

Marty: Well I know that you have a very, kind of, ritualized routine. For instance, you start the morning very early, you sit — well, tell us how you do start the day.

Nick: I love to get up in the morning. You know, some-times I'll write poems standing on my head.

Marty: Well, I know that [laughs].

Nick: I'm weird . . . George [Vallianos] says, "You're weird."You know, I am, but I'm tellin' you, look, the thing is this, though, what's good about standing on your head is you get 15 percent more brain power.

Marty: Can you feel that? I mean, do you feel your brain cells kicking in?

Nick: Who knows, who knows? A lot of this is talk about placebos, or whatever . . . but, I stand on my head, I take these old manuscripts, and I hope a word'll catch fire, and I'll write another poem, you know.

Marty: Are you meditating when you're on your head?

Nick: No, not really.

Marty: So you're just standing on your head?

Nick: I do yoga every day, that's what saved my life. Believe me, Hatha yoga's wonderful. And now I'm doing meditation, because I want to reduce my anxiety quotient, you know, so it won't affect my heart, and, uh, so forth. But, uh, I write in the bathroom. I'll take a shower and so forth, I'll have my manuscripts in there, and I'll stand upside down [laughter] . . . and look at the manuscripts, and then I'll go downstairs and sit cross-legs and go over it — I just love to do that because like Yeats said, you know, he had 15 years of delicious rewriting to do. Writing is rewriting. If it wasn't . . . my God — see, the mind is a wasteland, the mind is Eliot's wasteland. There's so much garbage out there, there's so much dead language. Every once in a while in this abandoned mine, you'll find a little nugget.

Marty: Hmmm.

Nick: A word or a line that'll trigger it, and set you on fire. Did you ever look at an Andrew Wyeth painting? You look at it and say, "Oh, it's representative," and then you look . . . and the thing catches fire.

Marty: And you find that with your writing?

Nick: Sometimes.

Marty: A word will do that?

Nick: Yeah.

Marty: . . . I read that you're more well known in Japan than you are in the States.

Nick: I don't know about that.

Marty: You don't know about that?

Nick: But they like my work.

Marty: Yeah.

Nick: Yeah, Kazuo Sato, he took the "lily" poem and translated it with the Crown Prince, and they said the poem's great, you know. And they say I'm great . . . so   . . . who's great? You know, if someone says your poem's immortal, you better burn it.

[laughter]

Nick: You know, really.

Essays by Nick Virgilio

A Journey to a Haiku
Nick Virgilio

In a corner of an old graveyard in Camden, N.J., there is
a small lot of bare, hard ground trampled by trespassers.
One day while passing by on a bus, I was impressed with
this lot which triggered a poetic experience that, in turn,
started trains of thought concerning the destined anonymity
of most human beings. One of the early attempts to
express the experience was:

the grassy graveyard . . .
  not a blade where children played,
    near the battleground

  This graveyard is not really "grassy." And "near the bat-
tleground" is a construct of the imagination. Some months
later, I imagined a poem with a plantation setting:

the plantation ruins:
  a bulldozer levels
    the slave quarters

  Somehow, a short time thereafter, the Camden grave-
yard experience began to fuse with efforts to compose
the "plantation" haiku. After several versions, I composed:

103

near the battleground
    where children play in the grass:
        the graveyard of slaves

Then the 'poem,' with one foot in Camden, N.J., and
the other on a southern plantation, planted both feet south
of the Mason-Dixon line:

near the battleground,
    where cattle graze in the grass:
        the grave mounds of slaves

After a few attempts to strengthen the weak second line
with either "where cattle graze in bluegrass," "where cattle
graze in waving grass," "where cattle graze in flowering
grass," or "where cattle graze in crab grass," I decided
it was impossible to really strengthen this line. I tried
rearranging the lines. As the poem evolved, I sensed that
"battleground" and "grave mounds" should be near each
other. This occurred after the change from "the graveyard
of slaves" to "the grave mounds of slaves." "Battleground"
and "grave mounds" is the major relationship; "cattle" and
"slaves" is of secondary importance.

    This, I think, is the best version; the "picture" and the
poem are improved:

where cattle graze
    near the grassy battleground:
        the grave mounds of slaves

The second and third lines suggest what is truly important:

near the grassy battleground:
    the grave mounds of slaves

"where cattle graze" justifies itself when the reader compares "cattle" to "slaves;" this line also introduces the peaceful mood of the poem.

Now consider the version that begins with "near the battleground." This line is vague, since it really doesn't put the reader in a *particular* place. And it could mislead the reader into thinking the war is still going on. "where cattle graze in the grass" is trite, compounded by the unnecessary "in the grass."

This second line acts as a barrier over which the reader must leap in order to connect "grave mounds" with "battle ground." In this version, the third line "the grave mounds of slaves" practically carries the entire load, and makes the poem. Of course, any poem should not depend for its very life on one line; the reader may lose interest before he gets to it.

Let us reexamine what I consider the best version:

where cattle graze
    near the grassy battleground:
        the grave mounds of slaves

We began with a real graveyard experience in Camden,

N.J., and transformed it into an imagined American historical "picture" haiku with a setting somewhere in the South. Thus, the journey takes us from a small lot of bare, hard ground to "the grave mounds of slaves," and destined anonymity.

On Haiku in English
Nick Virgilio

Are the poems below haiku? And do they fit the Japanese haiku tradition? This tradition is based primarily on the work of the four Japanese masters: Basho, Buson, Issa and Shiki.

a mossy willow,
　tossing in the autumn wind,
　　touches a tombstone

the misty woods:
　an uprooted hickory
　　bridges the brook

little brother's grave
　covered with dewy cobwebs –
　　he loved spiders

a voodoo drum
　echoing through the jungle
　　reflects the autumn moon

Let us begin by accepting Harold Henderson's definition of haiku: a record of a moment of emotion in which human nature is somehow linked to all nature. Mr. Henderson outlines the general characteristics of Japanese haiku in his book, *Haiku in English*, as follows:

• Consists of 17 Japanese syllables
• Contains at least some reference to nature (other than human nature)
• Refers to a particular event
• Presents that event as happening "now" — not in the past
• Emotion is conveyed not by stating or describing it, but by describing or clearly suggesting the circumstances that arouse it
• A quality of growth — an ability to convey more emotion than is experienced at a first reading

I believe my entries reflect these characteristics. However, in English it is impossible to consistently follow the Japanese form: 17 syllables (5-7-5) which are units of duration. I approximate a "form" that consists of 17 English syllables with sense or phrase-determined line breaks. The poet should never let the form attract attention away from the poem. An *approximation* is necessary for natural expression.

Like Buson, most of my haiku are "human-oriented" but nature is an integral part of each. This "human-oriented" approach often produces haiku-senryu, or pure senryu. However, I think this is the best approach to haiku for a Westerner rather than Basho's "nature-oriented" manner. To write like Basho, one must live as he did.

My work is clearly related to the Buson-Shiki School of Haiku. Adherents to this school consistently use the objective word-painting technique. They consciously employ the principle of internal comparison, and strive to realize the onomatopoeic potential of each poem. They also rely heavily on imagined reality, or a combination of real and imagined experience. If a poet uses the objective word-painting technique faithfully, Basho-type poems happen when they will happen.

Among my entries, the imagined reality of "a mossy willow" is the best example of this kind of poetry. It exemplifies line and poetic unity. The sound matches the sense. The willow, wind and tombstone are not compared by simile or metaphor but the differences and likenesses are equally important. This poem is "nature-oriented" and has growth quality. It is "clean" without any thought process on the surface and clear — the pictorial perspective is right.

The impressionistic "misty woods" is real experience. Here is an objective word-painting: the general "misty woods" is compared to the particular "an uprooted hickory bridges the brook." The "misty woods" is in harmony and contrast with the marriage of "hickory" and "brook."

The grim but delicate "little brother's grave" is reminiscent of the work of Issa, an example of haiku that contains the poet's thoughts and feelings as an integral part of the poem. This haiku is the quintessence of a true story. Three disparate objects are compared: little brother, a spider, and dewy cobwebs. All three exude a delicate quality, and all three have or will soon pass away.

"a voodoo drum" (imagined reality) transports us to a clearing deep in the Haitian jungle where a witch doctor practices sorcery. A sense of mystery and harmony (drum-jungle-moon) pervades this poem. The rhythm is good and the lines are further unified by assonance: *voodoo, through, moon*; *drum, jungle*; *echoing, reflecting*. A primitive "formal" religion blends with, and is compared to, the "informal" religion of nature.

These poems, which in my opinion fit the Henderson definition of haiku, reflect the general characteristics of the Japanese haiku and follow in the tradition of the Japanese masters, but are not imitations or Japanesque.

A Note to Young Writers
Nick Virgilio

Compose and study every day! Repeat . . . compose and study every day! Do write about what you know. If you live in the city five days a week, and visit the mountains on the weekend — don't just write about the mountains.

Be yourself, be natural; don't wear a robe and sandals or use a pseudonym; don't pretend to monkish austerity. In our culture, we are all more or less bourgeois. Remember: Basho lived it.

Please keep this in mind, you are not composing Japanese haiku but English poetry influenced by the Japanese haiku and its techniques. Do enter haiku contests; don't be afraid to lose: it's not so bad.

Eschew all false modesty!

A Tribute to Nick

A Tribute To Nick
Michael Doyle

The name Lawrence J. Virgilio entered my mind for the first time in January 1970, two-and-a-half years after he was killed in Vietnam on July 24, 1967. It was his death that eventually brought his brother, Nick, to the Sacred Heart Church community in Camden, where he became an enriching and delightful presence.

In January 1970, I led a Youth Mass at St. Joseph's Pro-Cathedral in Camden. The Vietnam War had been lengthening its trail of blood for 14 years. At one of the masses, I gave the name of a dead American soldier on an index card to each young person who entered the Church and asked him or her to stand when I would call the name. I called 300 names of soldiers killed in Vietnam, all from South Jersey. The name on my own card, a person unknown to me at the time, was Lawrence J. Virgilio. Four years later, while serving in St. Joan of Arc in Camden, I greeted an elderly couple who requested that a mass be offered for their son. I did not know them. The mother began to cry. The father said:

"We go through this every July."

I asked the name.

The mother said: "Lawrence J. Virgilio."

Astonished, I muttered, "Wait a minute."

115

Going upstairs to my room, I lifted an index card from an elevated position on my desk and brought it down. I laid it in front of them. It read: Lawrence J. Virgilio. Then, we all cried. This story was published in *The Catholic Star Herald*. Nick read it, called me immediately and came to Sacred Heart. I had never met him. The death of Larry Virgilio brought him and his haiku to the Sacred Heart community. It was a blessing for us and a blessing for him, because for the first time in his life, he had a large community into which he was welcomed and in which he was admired. He had an audience of many individuals on whom he could try out his latest arrangement of syllables, attend his readings and support him. Even in the mass, at the peace giving, he was known to often whisper a new haiku in a woman's ear. He was never dismayed by any less than an enthusiastic response. He was admirable in that regard. In a letter to a writer seeking his advice, he wrote: "Don't let anyone's opinion discourage you." He himself wrote continually. In the same letter, he said: "Whatever I have achieved has come of very hard work, study and composition since 1962."

A daily routine for Nick was boarding the bus to the Reading Terminal in Philadelphia. There, after he smelled the fruit and the fish, the breads and the bacon, he talked to people. Sometimes he'd start a conversation with, "Get a load a this!" as he tried out a haiku on a startled man or woman on a lunch break. Nick was an interesting combination. He was more spiritual than many monks as he sought truth in the "cell" of a cellar space at 1092 Niagara Road in Camden, where the Virgilio family had lived since 1939. I visited the "cell" and saw where he sat under a naked bulb by the washing machine. But Nick was also a forceful salesman, selling haiku with "a smile and a shoeshine," selling it for a word of approval. This master of haiku once sold encyclopedias in New York City. He hardly had five dollars in his pocket and yet he always looked good in the meager options of his wardrobe. As he often said: "I wear dead men's clothes."

On his return from the Reading Terminal, he stopped almost every day at Sacred Heart Rectory, where he washed the dishes, made tea and hit me with two haiku. I always marveled that this famous poet was washing the dishes and talking without stop in the kitchen. To this day, I miss him.

On the last Sunday of his life, he arrived at Sacred Heart Rectory at 10 a.m., where a couple of regulars were having coffee in the kitchen. He presented two new haiku. This time we all liked them. As I walked with him over to church, he said:

"You'll tell them about *Nightwatch?*"

"I will."

I always announced his coming events, but teased a bit

about them so as to prevent too many requests from others for announcements. This time I played with the late hour of CBS-TV's *Nightwatch*. But a feeling came over me that I was playing too much and I said:

"But all joking aside, Nick Virgilio, with his haiku, has mined beauty out of the gutters of Camden."

I went on with further praise. After mass, Nick was saying to people:

"Did you hear what Michael said about me?"

Outside, he grabbed my hand with shining eagerness. I never saw him again.

Two days later, on Tuesday, January 3, 1989, Dan Dougherty of Sacred Heart drove him to Washington for the taping of *Nightwatch* with Scott Simon, filling in for Charlie Rose. During the show came the heart attack and the rush to George Washington University Hospital. Nick died at 2:10 pm. On Thursday, I went to Washington with Frank Falco, an undertaker, to bring his body home. On the way back, I was totally silent in the station wagon while Frank smoked and listened to the radio. After a while, he asked:

"Did this man write a book?"

"Yes."

Frank had never heard of haiku. I explained as well as I could and recited a favorite of mine that is connected to the Depression from his book:

the sack of kittens
sinking in the icy creek
increases the cold

Immediately, Frank's hand pulled up the collar of his over-
coat higher on his neck and he audibly shivered. My heart
leaped with joy. Nick is alive.

On Saturday, his brother Tony, his relatives and his
beloved community of Sacred Heart gathered for his
funeral. His last resting place is Harleigh Cemetery
beneath a granite podium monument designed by the late
Bob McGovern. Two signs of similar size direct visitors to
his grave and the nearby mausoleum of Walt Whitman. "I
am not worthy to shine his shoes," Nick often said of Walt.
Now they are a shared destination in Camden, N.J.

Harleigh Cemetery, which was established in 1885, has
the graves and enormous monuments of the rich mer-
chants and powerful people of a former Camden, but
there is only one grave where many people gather every
year on the Sunday afternoon nearest to the date of his
birth, June 28, 1928. That grave is Nick Virgilio's. People
read their haiku at the sacred podium and eat the birthday
cake. It is organized by the Nick Virgilio Haiku
Association, which arose out of his Sacred Heart commu-
nity. The rich legacy of Nick Virgilio will always be
immeasurable inspiration.

We can only marvel at the "terrible beauty" that Nick brought forth from the tragedy of his brother Larry's death in Vietnam, poignant haiku that Cor van den Heuvel called "one of the finest elegies ever written." We can say, too, that good has come from that terrible day in Washington when Nick's hopes of celebrating haiku from coast to coast were dashed. We are reminded of other dashed hopes in Texas, when he lost his job in radio work. Radio was the life for which he prepared at Temple University in Philadelphia. Worse still was the break-up of a serious love relationship. A saddened, broken man drove home to Camden. He never drove again. The eruption in his life was seismic. Seeking solace in poetic readings, he found haiku and later the realization that with hard work, he could write it. It became a way of life. The discovery was like finding flowers growing in the lava of his great upheaval. Nick Virgilio found himself. He found a way to pour forth the beauty of his soul in magnificent haiku upon the world.

January 2012
Camden, N.J.

Photos

Anthony, Nick's father

Rose, Nick's mother

Nick, right, and Tony, his middle brother, to the left

PHOTOS

NICHOLAS A. VIRGILIO
1092 Niagara Road
General Education
Answers to: "Virg"
Initials: N. V. Translation: Nice Vocalist
Ambition: Engineer
Allergic to: Algebra
Remembered for: Dizziness

ARNOLD F. VOGEL
730 Tulip Street
College Preparatory
Answers to: "Baron"
Initials: A. V. Translation: Always Vigorous
Ambition: Beat the Bass Drum in the Salvation
Army
Allergic to: Wilson girls
Remembered for: Running the mile

Nick's high school yearbook

Nick's kid brother, Larry, in uniform

Nick at home in Camden

Nick in Dallas in the 1950s

PHOTOS

Nick with his parents in his later years

Nick is in the third row, second from right,
in this photo at Sacred Heart Church

Nick at a Sacred Heart celebration

Elgin diner in Camden at night

Nick at a haiku reading
at the Elgin Diner

Nick reading by Walt Whitman's tomb

A ceremony to mark Nick's reburial by Walt Whitman's tomb

The podium constructed by Nick's grave in Harleigh Cemetery

Acknowledgments

This project would never have come to fruition without the efforts of many people, but none more so than Tony Virgilio, who has worked tirelessly to keep alive his brother's memory and poetry. In addition, Raffael de Gruttola, the editor of this volume, wrote a fine introduction and read through countless poems that Nick left behind in order to select the best ones for this collection. Father Michael Doyle penned a moving tribute, provided family photos, and was a constant source of encouragement. Kathleen O'Toole contributed an insightful afterword and helped in numerous other ways. Michele Robinson assisted with myriad details as well. Support was also provided by Laura Ahearn, Edward Cialella, Toni Libro, Bonnie Squires and the members of the Nick Virgilio Haiku Association Board, including Theresa Banford, Henry Brann, Linda Delengowski, Father Michael Doyle, Mary Heron, Ben Hill, Walt Howat, Kathleen O'Toole, Robin Palley, Michele Robinson, B.J. Swartz, George Vallianos and Tony Virgilio.

Many thanks are also due to Dean Kriste Lindenmeyer and Professor Geoffrey Sill of Rutgers University at Camden for providing initial access to the Virgilio archives and for hosting an exhibition of Nick's papers at the Paul Robeson Library. And, finally, to all others too numerous to name who have provided encouragement and assistance along the way, we would like to express our deep appreciation.

Excerpts of the Marty Moss-Coane interview with Nick are reprinted by permission of WHYY, Philadelphia, Pennsylvania. The interview, which ran on her show, "Radio Times," was broadcast in the week prior to 12/22/88.

Most of the poems in this book have not been previously published; however, some have appeared over the years in the following haiku magazines, journals, and fine art presses: *American Haiku, Asphodel, Brussels Sprout, Cicada, Frogpond, Haiku West, Modern Haiku, R.E.M. / Art Press* and *Wind Chimes*.

Front cover: Linda Delengowski, who painted a mural of Nick's poem *rank grass* in the Fairview section of Camden, graciously allowed a photo of it to be used here.

Back cover: Photo taken and reproduced by permission of J. Kyle Keener.

Interior Photos: All of the family photos in the book are courtesy of Tony Virgilio and Father Michael Doyle. Elgin Diner photo and Nick's reading there is courtesy of George Vallianos.

Original Manuscripts: Photos taken by Rick Black with the permission of Rutgers University at Camden and reproduced by permission of Tony Virgilio.

132

Appendix

Original Manuscript Pages

thes-line shirt cuffing the boxer

thunderheads shroud a cloud of gnats

wood by the river...

ing its rhyme at the root,

a shrou

ting a shadow ashore.

a cloud of gnats shroud

the evening sun

grass

lown pampas plumes...

ter's torch licks the autumn moon -

ing hound.

There is no creativity without

experimentation

Dawn on the duty

n my parade !

the monarch

in the sunlit window -

ing butterflies

a buzzing-bouncing fly mixing mot

Down the ghetto street

glittering with broken glass -

a barefooted child.

The autumn moon
emerging from a murky cloud,
silhouttes a jet.

he cathedral,

The village flag

dark road alone

rippling in the April wind,

the cold wind.

hides the rising moon.

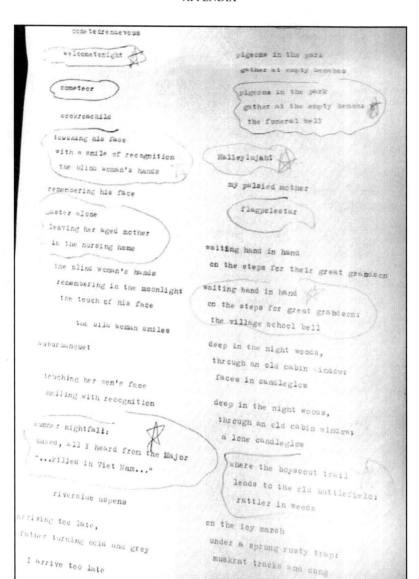

cometeorendezvous

welcometonight

cometeor

cockroachild

touching his face
with a smile of recognition
the blind woman's hands

remembering his face

Easter alone
leaving her aged mother
in the nursing home

the blind woman's hands
remembering in the moonlight
the touch of his face

the old woman smiles

arbourbanquet

touching her son's face
smiling with recognition

summer nightfall;
naked, all I heard from the Major
"...killed in Viet Nam..."

riverside aspens

arriving too late,
father turning cold and grey
I arrive too late

pigeons in the park
gather at empty benches

pigeons in the park
gather at the empty bench;
the funeral bell

Halleylujah!

my palsied mother

flagpolestar

waiting hand in hand
on the steps for their great grandson

waiting hand in hand
on the steps for great grandson;
the village school bell

deep in the night woods,
through an old cabin window;
faces in candleglow

deep in the night woods,
through an old cabin window;
a lone candleglow

where the boyscout trail
leads to the old battlefield;
rattler in weeds

on the icy marsh
under a sprung rusty trap;
muskrat tracks and dung

APPENDIX

D Company, 1st Battalion, 5th Marines
Que Son Valley: 3:30 AM, July 24th, 1967

In the valley in the darkness,
Company D was overrun
By a sudden wave of sappers -
Exploding mortars like the sun !

In the valley in the darkness,
Though outnumbered five to one,
Delta butted, knifed and booted;
Delta made the enemy run !

In the valley in the sunlight,
Among the rounded, numbered dead
Corporal Lawrence Virgilio
lies Corporal Virgilio
With shrapne in his head
Shrapnel in the back of his head.

137

24519074R00094

Made in the USA
Lexington, KY
21 July 2013